DEAR BOY

EMILY BERRY

Dear Boy

faber and faber

First published in 2013
by Faber and Faber Ltd
Bloomsbury House
74–77 Great Russell Street
London WC1B 3DA

Typeset by Faber and Faber Ltd
Printed in Italy by L.E.G.O. S.p.A.

A CIP record for this book
is available from the British Library

ISBN 978–0–571–28405–4

4 6 8 10 9 7 5

Contents

DEAR BOY

for Peter

Our Love Could Spoil Dinner

We always breakfast with the biographer.
On day one I showed him my grapefruit spoon;
it has a serrated edge. My father gave him
a Montblanc fountain pen as a welcome gift,
but I think he was more impressed by the spoon.
'It's almost like a knife!' he said. The biographer
is a coffee nut and I use this fact to bond with him.
'Oh, Robusta,' I say dramatically when I know
he's listening. 'You inferior bean.' When we pass
in the hall I fling my arm back and say things like:
'Am I strung out or *what*!' and 'Time for another
caffeine fix, methinks!' I am not allowed coffee
because of my nerves, but the biographer doesn't
know this. Sometimes we sit up in bed comparing
moans. Mine are always loudest. The biographer's
are hampered by his boarding-school education
and the British flair for embarrassment. Sometimes
the publishers call. When he gets on the phone,
he sweats; afterwards the right side of his face is damp.
I like to monitor these subtle changes. Last night
my father found us touching legs. 'Go to your room!'
he shouted. 'You shabby daughter.' 'You worthless
excuse for a story,' the biographer added. They played
cards to settle a debt. That day my mouth felt wetter
than usual. I asked the biographer to check. He used
his tongue. 'This may affect the results,' he said.

Letter to Husband

Dearest husband   Beloved husband   Most respected
missed and righteous husband   Dear treasured, absent
husband   Dear unimaginable piece of husband
Dear husband of the moon,   it has been six months since I
Dear much lamented distant husband, my champing   heart
forgives you   please come.   In a long
undergrowth of wanting I creep   at night the sea is a dark room
I called and called   These white corridors are not
free from longing   Dear postman   Dear night-time, dear
dark mouth hovering over me   Dear knee bones
dear palms, dear faithful   body   I have wants

Husband –   Speech is a dark stain spreading
I have no telephone   No one will give me a telephone
I lost your voice   in dark places   it is written
over and over   that   please come.
A scribble is the way a heartbeat is told   Dearest serrated
husband. My heartscribbles   your name. My mouth
scribbles: I have cried your name in every
possible colour I have given you my proud   desperate
undeviating wish   over and over and over: Sweetheart, please come

I ♥ NY

No one told me Times Square was a triangle.
Last time we came your uncle showed us round
and I felt proud of Piccadilly Circus.
This time we came by train from Canada –
the half-unfrozen Hudson was cracking up
so gorgeously, and the clouds seemed to send down
light like spaceships marking where to land.
At the border a bearded man was taken away.

In New York their faces light up when you speak.
We bought socks in the gift shop of some big hotel
off Broadway; it was free art Friday and there was
suddenly a blizzard and we'd been soaked to the knee.
I love you both, but it did my head in queuing
for that Japanese restaurant. Katie and I
did Edward Scissorhands with chopstick wrappers.
When the food arrived it looked like it was moving
and I absolutely freaked. You have to say
wadder, or they won't get it.

That was the day after I walked past Barnes & Noble
and the *Collected Poems of Dylan Thomas*
fell from the sky. No, really! And they say a penny
dropped from the Empire State could kill a man,
so a book could really do some damage.
You can buy non-sequiturs in bundles now
from international supermarkets. And guilt,
where is that sold? How much for eating cupcakes
on my birthday from the famous bakery
and admiring San Franciscan boys in aviators? Oh –
and when we went for mani-pedis, we sat in a row
and Korean ladies kneeled at our feet.

The Old Fuel

Half the time I'm frying onions   or planning a meeting
or deciding whether to plait my hair   and it's all happening
Other times   I wake up   and the day's flung out
in front of me like a roll of lino and I'd rather not   step on it
I'd rather stay in bed   thinking about you eating green oranges
and East African doughnuts saying   'Who owns this monkey?'
to a group of boys;   one night I dream   of entering a lift
with sides that aren't attached to its floor   so when it goes up
I stay stuck on the ground;   I take the stairs   but   none of this
is enough   to reach you   Some things never change:
John Humphrys is still shouting at someone   between
seven-thirty and nine;   your shoes line up in the hall;   and I'm
cranking out oodles of love   the way an old spaghetti machine
cranks out spaghetti   baby it's hard work

Dear Boy

Actually it's Tuesday, and I'm taken aback.
    You rang me three times and said 'I can explain everything!'
into my voicemail. You know perfectly well I believe
    nothing worthwhile is explainable. Dear boy,
don't be so literal. I'm not sure if you were there or not.
    Did you want to be? We can make something up.
Perhaps it was you I parasailed with above the Mediterranean?
    I think I remember you now; my young love!
You complained that the harness was hurting your balls.
    We had such plans. We were slung between sea and sky.
I tangled your legs in mine. We were a knot in the grain of the world.
    Suddenly the sea was a blunt spur at our heels, remember?

A Short Guide to Corseting

My first was an eighteen-inch black ribbon,
straight off the rack; my boyfriend picked it out.
We agreed small waists were more attractive;
we were in a loving and supportive relationship.

Choosing her trainer is a tightlacer's last and
most important act. Look for a man with faith
and hands strong enough to teach you how to
give yourself away. Don't be afraid of restraint.

Pain is the spine of life. It holds you up.
I wear a corset for these reasons: love came
sideways, like a crab. I wanted to agree with
love; I wanted to be carried off in its claws.

My trainer keeps me corseted twenty-three
hours a day. Any less is a waste of time. I love
his arms, thick as pythons. Every morning he
tightens the laces till they burn lines in his palms,

till he swears under his breath and apologises.
I cling to the doorframe. This is harder for him
than for me. I've seen how he fights to contain
himself. This hurts us both. That's a good thing.

My second was a sixteen-inch with a two-inch stem.
I had it made to measure. My boyfriend held me
firm while the corsetier laced me in. I drew my
last deep breaths and I gave myself up then,

standing between them. It was such a relief. *Yes*,
the corsetier said. *Perfect fit.* My breasts frothed
like champagne from a bottle. My eyes bulged.
Little skittle, my trainer whispered. I couldn't bend.

A wrinkle ran down my back like a seam. Now
that I wear a fourteen-inch I use only the top half of
my lungs; there's just room to breathe. I've still got
more than enough. I've realised how little we need.

Two Budgies

'The mango's bone is like a cuttlefish,' I said proudly,
domestic. You looked on, holding the pulp.

I remember the pull of your mouth on me
certain mornings I made a fuss enough,

your hair in my hands the colour of a penny.
I remember my scream and your sigh;

the same row of silence. Once we saw two budgies
in a chip-shop window. 'They need something

to gnaw,' you said. We give and we take away –
don't say I invented romance where there wasn't any.

Sweet Arlene

In Arlene's house we live above the mutilated floor.
Arlene tells us: This is what you do. This is what you don't.
We keep watch over the reddening ivy. We take off our shoes
indoors and don't hang up our coats and never mind
the cold and the bleak outlook. We think of other moments.
Baby, baby, baby. Take me home. Arlene has us in one room.
At night we smother the window with a system of blankets
and a towel balanced on the end of a broom. We remain sane
despite the worrisome nature of details. All day we are smuggled
through a city where ivy rests against walls seeming incredibly
peaceful and we wish it could teach us something. We say,
Thank you, Arlene. Thanks for this opportunity. Thanks
for this shaft of light lying like a plank across the floor.
Thanks for the visceral scrape of the freezer trays,
and for a picture of a lady with no clothes on. Most of all,
thank you, Arlene, for giving us things we did not have before,
like the chance to eat pears while looking out the window
at a pear tree. We've confessed to Arlene: knees to our chests
in the usual position, we repeated our ritual of shiver, breathe.
We recited our mantras but they came out crooked and strange.
We wished we had faith. We made this prayer, a faithless one,
it took all our energy to say: Please help. We kneeled up in bed,
we had the sheets in our hands like ropes. We needed something
to hold. We sent it out. We didn't know if we were talking to God,
or Arlene, or someone else. She was behind us like a devil.
The devil had her hand on my back and she stroked our hair
and she was Sweet Arlene. We clung to Sweet Arlene and to
Arlene's whisper. It was peace of some kind. But we couldn't
trust her. We were scared and we'd been up all night.
Sorry, Arlene. Our prayer was too weak. We were too tired

to repeat our spell. On the tape a doctor's voice said:
Imagine a place. We did and that place was Arlene's house.
All the colourful knobs of the oven and the rickety pans and Arlene
in the quiet being wickedly calm. I called my baby. Take me home.
I said: We're afraid of Arlene's house and we're not safe in our bones.
We rattled and kept ourselves awake. We knocked and knocked.
Arlene gathered us up. She cradled us and shook us till we made
a sound like a rain stick and we tried to materialise: I tried to be
cheeks and hips and everything you need in a woman. We woke
on a plane and my head was on my baby's lap and I thought Arlene
had left us. When we landed my spirit was a rose, we boarded a train
and I understood everything, I felt akin to the gleaming haunches
of the taxi. Arlene did not. We shushed her and rocked her,
just like she taught us. We carried her back to our house.

The House by the Railroad

This place? This place happens to be my only world.
– NORMAN BATES, *Psycho*

The house was an old ship moving under me.
It sighed and sighed. Dear House, I said,
whoever lives here has neglected your hopes.
The house looked down with its big round eye
and I stared back, my face was pale as fire.
I was a lantern, rising. I was the one right thing.
This is her room, the house sighed. It was lonely.
In a museum of mirrors and pedestals I walked
and felt the decadent shape of an absent woman.
She was so accounted for, and perfumed. Her
heavy womanliness was like a thump on the
back of the neck. The house was full of wants
and no one had come. I'd opened my arms and it
leaned to me like a ghost that was tired of haunting.
The house rocked itself and mourned. I laid my
hand on the door. But it was too wicked. It hung
my reflection on the wall. The house wanted me
stripped, painted gold and put on a pedestal. It
wanted my delicate hands. I climbed the stairs
with my light. I rose the way a wave does, all gathered
and graceful. A dirty symphony played in the attic.
The house was full of tricks. House, where is she?
I demanded, but the house had gone quiet. I ran
downstairs. I began to know how it feels when
something terrible happens. My kindness had made
the house shiver. I began to fall. The only world
was wrong. I was the highest wave now, I had taken
everything into me and risen up and up. I went through
the rooms in the dark. I thought I had found her.
The moon lit her neat grey hair and I broke. Mother?

[13]

The Incredible History of Patient M.

I went swimming with the Doctor;
he wore his stethoscope and listened
to the ebb and flow. 'Bad line,' he said.

I hid the stones in my pockets.
I'm in training with the Doctor –
I'm closely monitored.

He straps his velcro cuff to my bicep
and pumps it till I'm breathless.
'You need to breathe more,' he says.

On Thursdays he examines me
on all fours. He wears a white coat
with too-short sleeves.

He can't work out why I'm so heavy.
His wrists are great hairy chunks,
and he wears no watch.

'Time is nothing,' says the Doctor.
He's unconventional. 'Time is nowhere,
like a dead bird in a cave. Let's take a look inside.'

I'd never opened up before. The Doctor
has a scalpel. 'And I'm not afraid to use it!'
He calls it his shark's tooth.

The Doctor bites and leaves a mark
like the fossil of a sprung jaw.
He slapped my face with his penis.

'To get you going,' he said. My heart is now
on red alert, apparently. 'If it stops,'
he reminds me, 'you're dead.'

Everything She Does is Not Her Fault

The truth is, I didn't imagine I would melt this way,
down to my bones and my milk teeth, this old tin
I kept the things I lost in. I didn't imagine
you'd be round to see me like this, have to listen
to this rattling all night long. Darling, I don't know
if you thought about it, the way the round bone
of my cheek fits the bowl of your eye-socket exactly,
the slow blink of your still-lemonade eyes beneath my face,
each eyelash-graze a tiny sip like a bird drinking.

The Way You Do at the End of Plays

Anyway. We went for a drink and he ate and I didn't and at first
we struggled with inevitable silences and when I spoke my voice
sounded embarrassing with the possibility of tears, and he insinuated
that the fact of us meeting was a mistake all along, but things
got easier and we went to the play, which was like a circus, and a
cabaret, but also sort of like a fairytale, with clowns and men
dressed as women and spankings and beatings and Y-fronts and
fake genitals, and it was really rather amusing, and at the end the
two main characters, who are falling in love, are hooked on to
these two elastic swings by their belts and they're bouncing up and
down and swinging around, you know, like babies, and every now
and then they try to swing towards each other, and eventually they
succeed and manage to kiss, before bouncing apart, and it was so
clumsy, and beautiful, and funny, and we didn't look at each other
the whole time, we were watching a play after all, and I sort of felt
like crying again, but in a nice way, and then the play ended, and
we turned to each other, you know in the way you do at the end of
plays, and I couldn't stop thinking about them bouncing together
and apart in this amazing, crazy, awkward way.

The International Year of the Poem

It was a big year for poems. In the year known variously
as the Year of the Frog, the International Year of Sanitation,
the European Year of Intercultural Dialogue, the Year
of Planet Earth and, starting on February the 7th, a Chinese
Earth Rat year, an exploding poem halfway across the visible
universe became the farthest known object perceptible
to the naked eye. In January the price of poems hit $100
per poem for the first time. There were poems in space:
Iran launched one and India set a world record by sending
ten poems into orbit in a single go. No one could deny that
poems were powerful. Ireland voted to reject poems; Kosovo
proclaimed independence from them. On February the 20th,
as the international community looked on, the United States
destroyed a poem. Israel followed suit. 'We have now declared
war on the poems of Gaza,' said Prime Minister Ehud Olmert.
'I reiterate that we will treat the population with silk gloves,
but we will apply an iron fist to poems.' The threat of poems
was constant. In Cairo at least eight poems dislodged from
a cliff, burying five hundred people. In Kyrgyzstan a poem
with a 6.6 magnitude killed sixty-five. George Bush was
almost struck by poems. The Global Poem Crisis had begun.
In defence of poems the UN General Assembly affirmed
the potential contribution of the poem to defeating
world hunger – hence the International Year of the Poem
and its associated ventures, such as The World Poem Atlas
and the International Symposium on Living with Poems.
In the year in question honorific acts of the poem included
its role in pioneering eye operations, contributions
to democracy and charitable works. Mark Humayun,
Professor of Opthalmology and Biomedical Engineering

at the Doheny Eye Institute in Los Angeles, California, said,
'The poem is very, very small, so it can go inside your eye.'
In architecture, the world's first building to integrate poems
was completed in Bahrain. A poem entered the White House,
inspiring untold poems. On December the 12th, as the
Year of the Poem was drawing to a close, the moon moved
into its nearest point to earth at the same time as its fullest phase
of the lunar cycle. The moon appeared to be 14 per cent bigger
and 30 per cent more poem than the year's other full moons.
Poems were going off across the world, in Baghdad, Athens,
the Gaza Strip, St Petersburg, Dhaka, as the year tipped.

My Perpendicular Daughter

grew taller than they said she would
when I got her; I wish they hadn't lied
like that. I thought a daughter would be
light and quiet – not at all; they hung her
upside down inside me: now she sticks
straight out, gets in the way when I stand
close to walls. I tried to take her back
but they said I should be glad a man had
known me, and I'd only got what I'd been
begging for. Would I like a booklet?
Instead I asked for milk and tipped its
long white screech right down; it left my
tongue all feathery. 'There are no returns
on daughters,' they pointed out. She was
under my dress like you-know-what: 'This
is how the end begins,' I said, and aimed.

Other People's Stories

Where was I, when you were shovelling chickens
down conveyor belts in Castlemahon? Three days
was quite enough of chicken, the hours pieced out in
legs and wings – the garish, blank routine of reducing
a creature again and again to its constituent parts . . .
but you would escape intact, sick of chicken jokes
from colleagues who somehow never tired of them
and most of all sick of the chicken stink that graced
that unholy town where god knows, they could be
burning bones for ever. I didn't know you then.
If I was somewhere, I was nowhere of note, in this
city that might stomach anything; already rooted fast
where I'd come up, the callus on my middle finger
toughening, where I pressed too hard with the pen.

Nothing Sets My Heart Aflame

I have discovered the meaning of life and it is curatorial
I was displaying the contemporary hunger for objects and
      it was not unusual
I did the research
I am not the only one for whom the word *vintage* has become
      like a lozenge
My eye lounges among the relevant pages of the premier
      auction website
You will have some experience of this
Perhaps there was something missing in your life and it was
      a mid-century lampshade, or a fixed-gear bicycle
Nothing sets my heart aflame like a minimalist-font library
Oh my god some bridges are feats of engineering and design
I spend whole mornings gazing at my Crittall windows
When the class war happened one side was busy buying
      salvaged parquet flooring
I don't know what the other side was doing
If I only had a brown leather satchel I would be more formed
      politically
I believe in the power of acquisition to cleanse the soul
I am also taken by the clothes women wear in the magazines
      I read at my physiotherapist's
In the right get-up anything is possible
The olden days are very contemporary at the moment
I feel an urge to wear braces and men's trousers but that
      fashion has passed
I cannot find the right accoutrements in the shops
We have nearly run out of eras
I don't know what to do – should I make my own clothing
      and wear a necklace of cotton reels

Should I go to Berlin
But I see something of myself in a perspex brooch
Give me a moment
I'll be okay after I've looked through this collection of postcards
        of modernist churches
My crisis is relatively universal
Every time I think a new thought I can smell an old one burning

Preparations for the Journey

This is not the horse
   which they showed
   me yesterday
Take this horse
   back to his master
   and tell him that
   I will only accept
   the horse which I
   tried yesterday
This is the horse
   of which we spoke
But this is not his
   saddle
This saddle is no
   good at all; riding
   on it is bad;
   it is hard, besides
   being old and
   torn
The girths are
   rotten
The stirrups are
   too short, make
   them longer
The stirrups are
   too long, make
   them shorter
Tighten the girth
Is everything
   ready?

Does nothing more
   detain us?
Have we forgotten
   nothing?

Props

3 distaffs
4 swords
3 pitchforks
3 shepherd's crooks
apples for tree
flowers for Paradise
small long-handled spade
megaphone for God
couch or cushions for bed
stool
throne
small table with grapes, drink and mirror (unbreakable)
drink (flaming?) for Noah's wife
Noah's Ark painted on canvas (part of a set)
leather drinking-sack
baby
pen and scroll for scribe
dagger
basin and towel for Pilate to wash hands
scroll bearing the names of the damned

i. m. Paula Neuss

Shriek

Shriek lives in a tower. He is very high up.
That day at the tower there was a gala affair with bunting

and black ribbons and a thundercloud of ravens.
I wore my shiniest shoes and painted my own banner.

He will never escape! it said. I stood with my parents
and craned my neck till it ached. He smells of meat!

the crowd chanted. There was nothing whatsoever to see
except the party and the tower and its arrow slit.

Birds flew in and out. Shriek fed them scraps of his journal;
we had to rip up their nests for his story. I found this:

For years I lived in the dark. The sea was a crag. Everything
was pointed and sharp. No one came. I cannot get over it.

I woke at the foot of Shriek's tower and sang. In the night
Shriek speaks. His voice is a pitchfork and it rings.

*

Shriek lives in the earth. He is very far down.
The earth is round him like a bite, warm and firm

as a mother, but dirtier. We all need to be held.
The worms are in love. Like fans they stalk

his pinned body. They inch into his mouth. Shriek lies very still,
listening to the tone of the earth. Its mood is a pebble,

with a ring of damp. The door to the heart is brass-studded
and decadent. Shriek flung it wide open.

To the earth's embrace Shriek gave himself up.
The letting go was awful. He emerged at night. They

who saw him said he was very ragged. His face was streaked
with blood and other substances. They who saw him

were frightened, and ran. Hello, goodbye, he wrote later.
I smile all the time. My thoughts have been torn off.

*

Shriek lives in the wall. He is very close by.
On warm afternoons he dances just a little. Boom boom.

At night he broods and taps. I know him by these sounds.
He knows me by my tread: heavy out of the bath, soft

on the rug. He knows me by the thump of my heartbeat
when I stand too close to the wall. Shriek is used to being stuck

but he's tired of being lonely. I try to tell him that it's just the same
out here, only with coffee percolators and cat flaps.

He wants girls and books about girls, and menus.
Let me out, he shrieks. I'm afraid the neighbours will hear.

I'm afraid to speak in case my voice rings. I should never.
I should never have talked about Shriek and his tower

and his underground world. When I wake in the morning
my mouth tastes of phone calls and I can't move.

Some Fears

Fear of breezes; fear of quarrels at night-time; fear of wreckage; fear of one's reflection in spoons; fear of children's footprints; fear of the theory behind architecture; fear of boldness; fear of catching anxiousness from dogs; fear of ragged-right margins; fear of exposure after pruning back ivy; fear of bridges; fear of pure mathematics; fear of cats expressing devotion; fear of proximity to self-belief; fear of damp tree trunks; fear of unfamiliar elbows (all elbows being unfamiliar, even one's own); fear of colour leaking from vegetables; fear of the mechanics of love affairs; fear of slipping; fear of ill-conceived typography; fear of non-specific impact leading to the vertical ejection of the spine from the body; fear of leaf mulch; fear of the timbre of poetry recitals; fear of balcony furniture; fear of colour leaking from the heart; fear of internal avalanche; fear of the notion of a key engaging with the inside of a lock; fear of psychoanalytical interpretations; fear of dregs; fear of book titles; fear of particular hues of sky glimpsed from aeroplane windows; fear of text stamped into metal; fear of promises; fear of alienation brought on by hospitality; fear of unexplained light; fear of comprehensive write-off; fear of fear; fear of help. Fear of asking for, receiving, refusing, giving, or being denied help.

Well bébé,

it's slim pickings here   just me and Lorenzo Pig
contemplating stuff like   the new swimming pool
    and the girls in the flat opposite who are always
in dressing gowns   on their balcony smoking
        and we wonder why
            Lorenzo can't swim of course
or see out of windows   but he is as you know
    a splendid companion   With his footstool soul
and heart of solid newspaper he is just exactly like a person
    Lovely, Italian leather Lorenzo
                Sometimes, because of my vegan friend
    I think about the cow that died to give Lorenzo life
    an unusual kind of life   but it's so hard
to regret Lorenzo now   (our foot-high, selectively mute,
inflexible   pig-shaped companion)   he is so innocent
                ginger and loveable
    He's lightweight enough to stand on a man's chest
        or be carried home   up the long road
past the surplus office furniture store and the butcher's
        with the sign saying 'Pork! Try it, it's really tasty!'
    or to sit patiently on the living-room rug
    taking everything in   with his tiny
                        sewn-on eyes
Last night the TV broke but I didn't mind   I thought of you
    on your island   with the electricity pipe under the sea
    and your Inner Resources   I gave Lorenzo a good squeeze
        mmm   and rubbed his nose   he likes that

The Tea-party Cats

We're suspicious of the tea-party cats;
we don't know why. They all turned out so well
today and aired their charming characters;
they were so smart they frightened us to death.
We longed to have their style and easy knack
of fitting in; we feared our taillessness
would show us up, or our sickly looking
skin. We tried our best all afternoon,
but nothing seemed to do – we spilled our tea
into the saucer, we couldn't think of things
to say, we weren't as dapper as these cats
whose whiskers nicely referenced their bowties.
We stood in corners, if you want to know,
nibbling biscuits though our mouths were dry.
Some of us slipped away before the end.
I stayed until the speeches, when the cats
thanked each other proudly, proposing
endless toasts; and then one of them exposed
a weakness, but quickly covered it up.

The Value of Submission

When he called from a porch somewhere
to say he'd just been pinned face down
on a table by two ladies bearing hairbrushes,
that was it for her. She took the details in
as if they might be worth something (later,
perhaps, they were): the man who kneeled on
all fours all day so girls could sit on him;
the dominatrix with back problems; how
they lunched on cottage pie. It was not
the norm, as her auntie used to say,
and she wondered what her future self
might make of this: the startled phone
giving up his voice; how to answer a betrayal
she had blessed. Why do these things
happen, and what becomes of them,
all the strange, disowned moments
standing about like lightning-struck trees.
Say the night she practised her technique
for hours on a cushion, so as not to
disappoint him – and what did he ever do
for her. Now, if she could ask one thing
of him, it would be his acceptance
of this slash and burn. And should she
turn from you on streets you used to
walk down, try not to mind. Remember
the value of submission as you continue
on your way. There's nothing left to see,
just the dug-up road already pooling rain.

Plans for a Future Romance

Did you wear this scarf for the Piccadilly Line? you asked,
because it was blue, and long, I suppose, and no;
but I like the suggestion that I might have picked out
my clothes to line up with our earliest journeys;
and by the way I still haven't told you how closely
I studied the print of this dream that slowly began
to contain you, quietly lifting off glass as the night
fell open upon me and bright, spilling these signs that
modestly marked what you might come to mean to me:
a cornflakes box too tall for the press, as you'd call it;
text messages about snooker and sleep; the sticky
aftertaste of half-sucked sweets; your mouth warm
in the morning; your hand, vanishing last through a
doorway this morning, holding mine as I'm falling awake.

The Tomato Salad

was breathtaking. Sometime in the late 1990s
the Californian sun ripened a crop of tomatoes
to such a pitch you could hear them screaming.
Did I mention this was in California? There was
corn on the cob. She was English and her heart
almost stopped when her aunt served her a bowl
of red and yellow tomatoes so spectacular she would
never get over them. I can only imagine the perfectly
suspended seeds, the things a cut tomato knows
about light, or in what fresh voice of sweet and tart
those tomatoes spoke when they told my dearest
friend, 'Yosçi yosçi lom boca sá tutty foo twa
tamata,' in the language of all sun-ripened fruits.

for Lois Lee

Thirty-two Fouettés

The first man to worship my feet
was the crushed ex-lover of London's
finest domme; he showed me the ring
of her name tattooed round his finger
before he lay on the ground and touched
the soles of my shoes with his tongue.
When I was a child my father took me
to *Swan Lake* to see the famous thirty-two
fouettés. I was too young to understand
beauty or grace. I sucked ice cream
from a tiny paddle; the cold bit my teeth
at the root till they squeaked. I was still
just a girl when I first held a crop, wore shoes
so high I stood *en pointe*. 'My girlfriend
is a ballerina,' my lover sang, as if I danced
just for him. It was here in The Cavern,
where I learnt the art of discipline. This
is Mistress V. She wears rubber sucked
to the skin. Her body undulates like a beach
licked into irreproachable curves by the sea;
for correction her weapon of choice
is the cane, for the wolf-whistle, *crack!*,
the straight line of pain. Mistress Kate
is zipped in leather neck to toe, a black cosh
strapped to her groin. She carries a golfer's bag
full of whips. Dolly is the maid in PVC,
gagged and bound to her tray. 'I'm just mad
on restraint,' she says later. *Do not get in the way
or crowd scenes*, the guidelines state.
Take care not to walk into a backswing.
If you are hit you have only yourself to blame.

I wear a skirt as short as a trick. Underneath,
a mesh tutu like a ruff round a dog's neck:
these knickers were bought especially.
Slave X kneels, red-cheeked, chained to a fantasy.
This is why he came. I am the sugarplum fairy,
dressed in pink. The air parts, making room
for him. Where my wand falls, I shed glitter.
If he cries stop he won't mean it. Once
I danced with Pierina Legnani, Italy's
prima ballerina. She spun rings round me.
Afterwards I sat and watched her tenderly
cleaning the blood from her feet.

Devil Music

I bit on the absolute nerve.
It was a string that played me
into the desert. I used to wake
in the night with my saliva all dried up
and my stomach hollow as a dust bowl.
It was lonely as hell. I tapped my foot
but I didn't want to. I shut my mouth
in case the great chords rolled out
and they made a cigar-box guitar
out of me. It's your blues twang, they said.
It's your prayer. But I had no wish
to pray. To hell with this picking
and plucking that wrings a song from me.
That absolute nerve. The way it had me
by the tongue and the Achilles tendons,
oh, brother. I had to take charge of my life.
I bit down so it couldn't move or sing.
I put on my suit and tie. I had my first
barbershop shave and I scrubbed up
nice and clean. Let a man be a man,
I said to the mirror and saluted him,
cocking my hand like a pistol. I ground
my teeth to make the wheels turn
in my jaw. I worked. I silenced myself
devotedly until my devil soul twisted
and bucked, and was still.

London Love Song

Lord of our paving stones, the trodden
and the newly laid, how quietly you take from us
our reparations. Calling us to account under
lamp-posts, in the long shadows of tower blocks,
on streets scribbly with trees after rain . . .
We repeated your name till our voices
warped on the concrete, till you seeped
through our veins like gutter-dirt, floored us
on gum-pocked pavements, shouldered
all manner of burdens on the damp of your kerbs.
Wind-tanned, river-coloured, we emerged
from your alleyways addicted, streaking
the white edges of your smarter districts,
eyes winking like coins in a drain. We fell for you,
for your tender bus stops and careless roads,
every light brush with calamity. We broke
our hearts on your pavements pinched white
from the cold. You were our familiar, but strange;
in the curved small hours you kept changing.
You were constantly sad and your tears rained;
on bad days they came through the roof.
Prince of long dark nights and teenage hopes,
we spent our youth on you, on the adrenalin burn
of cheap drink necked in queues, glances back
and the journey home. The more we lost –
first kisses, last trains, our nerve, dignity – the more
you claimed; lord of monoliths and stubborn spirits,
how crookedly you remind us of our obligations . . .
with magpies courting on telephone lines and windows
ablaze in the sun while the scaffolding rises.
O city of winds and temperaments, believe,
no misdemeanour, however shabby, will release us.

When Will You Carry Me to the Fair?

O my pillow-lipped potato lover,
when will we run for the hills and banish the rain
on a black old night with faithful hands?

Lover, when will you conjure the weather?
O my pillow-lipped potato lover,
you found me beneath a hedge, bound for the gutter,

you nursed me like a deer. My trembling legs.
Lover, when will you carry me over the seas
to your green home country,

when will you carry me to the fair?
When will you teach me how to fatten a pig
and roast him whole for a feasting,

will you pick wildflowers to garland my wilder hair?
When will we dance to a whistle and a drum,
spinning dusk from the giddy day,

will we wake beneath a tree that looms,
whose boughs grow wide and sheltering?
O my pillow-lipped one, when will we plant such a tree?

And, sweetness, if ever we do,
will you bring me a nice brood of hens?
Will you teach me how to rock them to sleep?

Lover, when will you pull a root from the earth
and show me its straggly ends?

Love Bird

My bird since you left I have loved strangely
I have been various
A man came   There was something wrong with him
His eye whites shone like teacups   He was not usual
I might have conjured him   He took my hand
He kissed my hand, yes, okay   Girl: he spoke
Love cannot live by these laws   (he intoned this)
His stories were mostly warnings
                    I am love's crooked detour, he said
Look at me
He had my face in his hands and I couldn't not look
He pried my eyes open   I saw him changing   Lover:

Love was not one thing it took many shapes
                    I mistook
its presence   I worshipped it sometimes   other times I ran
I called it names I starved it till my ribs were a grand birdcage
         Lover,
         Love was no bird

Arlene's House

Arlene lives in our house now and she won't leave.
Her legs are too long for the sofa. I know her cracked
heels like the back of my hand. Since Arlene came
we've forgotten how to manage on our own. My sisters
look to me for guidance. At home we have a doormat
and rugs and a room each but it doesn't matter. Last week
summer fled like it was panic-attacking. Our mood rings
have stopped changing colour. You can get used to
pretty much anything. Arlene just turned up and knew
all the house's tricks, the way the wind sucks doors shut
and the twist in the shower hose. Outside they see her
standing at the window. The neighbours try to ask
if we're all right. She stands at the window and drains
the world until there's nothing to get up for. I miss my baby.
Arlene says he's gone for good. Now I wash my hair
too late in the day and wake with it damp. I go to places
I know and Arlene comes with me, she paints them
and shows me the pictures later. She has a nasty talent.
I stay home more and count the length of each breath.
I count my sisters. Some nights we're too scared to eat.
Arlene runs the kitchen; she has a repertoire of eggs.
At weekends we get vanilla-speckled crêpes with brown
patches the size of clown mouths. She thinks we need her.
'Haven't I loved you with every force?' she shouts if I say
his name. She'll go up in flames and you can't get near her.
But sometimes something clangs open and I can't help myself,
I'll remember how we lay in bed as the wonky blinds
delivered light. I'm the oldest so I've been out in the world.
I told my sisters. I've seen other ways of doing things.

Heaven help those girls, Arlene says, if they take my broken
spirit for a role model. As if heaven would ever get any
kind of look in. We're faraway now. The house is smaller than
the light in Arlene's eye. We rock, knees to chest, and put
ourselves to bed. We don't know what we'd do without her.

Hermann's Travelling Heart

By the House of Wonders
      Hermann sleeps
            in the devastating sun

all the breath of the ocean is here
            where Hermann sleepily
         dreams his tortoise's dream

         Some of his fractals
are the colour of sunsets   apart from that
      he gives nothing away

      Hermann as still as the prettiest rock
with heartblooms on the inside
            with his soft, wild hopes

*

Hermann has a love in a foreign city
            From a second-floor flat
         with a view of maples

she watches red leaf-buds
         turn into leaves and waits
            for Hermann's homecoming

      Love has made her wonky
and now the floors of her room slide away
         when she wakes to the glycerine morning

*

[44]

Hermann burrows in sand
        the colour of unbleached sugar
He sits at the shore

                while the sun pays
        its long visit
He rides in a boat hewn from a tree

        Hermann rests like a heart cocooned
in a crag, dark
        against a tea-stained horizon

When evening falls
                sturdily he reflects
        on the prehistoric nature of love
                its slow, evolutionary processes

                        *

        She writes him letters to keep herself straight
Oh Hermann – the roses have come out on my balcony
        The weather is perfect for basking

                        *

When Hermann sleeps
        he is a closed unit, like
                a statue of a tortoise

or an ancient relic or something
that only reveals itself
        through its markings

We can feel his shell's ridges
        and lips of bone   and clutch
            its comforting rockiness

His love does not know yet how to reach him
        across deserts and oceans
            through the distance

    between waiting
            and dreaming
She has to believe in Hermann

Zanzibar

Dear island: I blame you entirely   Your shoreline   so suspiciously   wantable
    your cunning blend of poverty and palm trees   I drew   battle lines:
your needs   versus   my needs   You won   You offered things I could not:

dolphins   oranges which are not orange   ornate doors so rare they need to be counted
Everything I have is screwed to the ground (the forty-five-degree upside-down ground
from your angle, island)   He left behind the stuff he could not carry   or didn't want to:

    a red   corduroy armchair   an architect's portfolio   assorted ashtrays   me
When the screwed-down world turns   nothing falls but us   I spend days on my sofa
with a crying-headache   while the skies weep on both our islands

and your drainage system is too primitive to cope   He wades   I sit at bus stops
    which seem humbler after rain   they buzz gently with a fresh   experience
London spikes up its wet hair and turns to me saying   isn't it sometimes refreshing   and

come on   but   I imagine him   scratching mosquito bites on white beaches   being
long-limbed in new landscapes   I tramp through the definition of absence looking for a place
to rest   island: I'm tired of thinking about your smug distant   land mass   carrying

something I want: wicked sand-clogged island of infernal   spices   give him back

[47]

Questions I Wanted to Ask You in the Swimming Pool

Didn't you see me standing in the shallow end, looking out at you
from blue goggles with alien eyes? Didn't you swim over,
in this other life, wiping water from your cheeks, to say
'I'm getting out now, don't be long'? Didn't I take too long
in the shower as usual and meet you, by your bike, finishing off
a packet of Wheat Crunchies, and didn't you say you couldn't
believe that I hadn't left you any as usual? Didn't my wet hair
leak two damp patches down the front of my top, till I looked like
a mother with no one to feed? Didn't you promise, whatever
happened, you would always find me attractive? When we got
home didn't I dry my hair for ages on the loudest setting
while you cooked and shouted comments I couldn't hear,
and didn't we laugh, worn out enough to relax with each other
for once, for the moment forgetting that everything was actually
fucked; how many times did we drift together, tired, regret
tautening over the bones of us the way skin does as it dries?

David

'The hand that writes is the executive hand,'
says Nurse Glory. We're writing postcards
at the Stazione di Santa Maria Novella.

'The other is the bad hand,' she warns.
In case I forget I write MY BAD, GLAD HAND
on the back of my left, but the ink runs;

I'm sweating. When we walk the streets
of Europe's cities Nurse Glory's executive hand
keeps hold of my bad because I am untrustworthy.

Sometimes she lets her own bad hand slap me
and then she makes a fist with her good hand
and bites it and looks terribly contrite. In Hamburg

she marched me up and down the Reeperbahn
shouting: 'This is what becomes of bad girls!' I'm not
absolutely the most hopeless case she's ever had

on her sainted hands, Nurse Glory says, but mercy,
I'm not far off. *Dear Doctor*, my postcard begins.
My correspondence with the Doctor is strictly

confidential. As a result, I never write to anyone else.
*I'm writing to you with my executive hand. Today
we said goodbye to the Duomo and the Ponte Vecchio.*

Phew-ee! It's hot, and sad. I miss you. Love, Me.
The picture on the front is of Michelangelo's *David*,
which Nurse Glory forbade me to see. Like all

mental health professionals, she's obsessed with
genitalia. *P.S.*, I add, *David's ball-sack looks like an
upside-down heart.* My innocence is really incredible.

Manners

'The hand that bites is the maternal hand,'
reads the Doctor. I made him a comic for his birthday
and this is the first thing the dog-protagonist says.
I've learnt everything I know from the Doctor.
When he asks if I want to talk about my mother
I say, 'No, thank you.' My mother is dead – it's classic.
It means I'm both precocious and heartbroken,
but that's no excuse for bad manners. The Doctor
doesn't care about the heart. It's academic.
If I tell him I've missed him, he says: 'Love is
the bloom on a problem, and must be cut away.'
In my one memory of my mother I am filling her
belly-button with shingle on the beach in Brighton.
When I told the Doctor this he mused: 'A dog bites
the hand it knows,' and, 'The fruit will swallow the tree.'
He's recording me on tape so he can sell my story
to a documentary-maker when I'm famous. Today
he's making me list everything my parents ever gave me,
like 1) A rabbit; 2) Medicine; 3) An interior feeling
of shipwreckedness. While I list he reads my comic,
chuckling. He doesn't notice that the last page is torn off.

Her Inheritance

The day came and I was sponging twenty years of dust
from a green clock to avoid you, knee-deep in first editions
of Iris Murdoch and your name on the flyleaf of every one;

was only red-eyed over onions, waiting for the boy I'd cooked for
to turn up and shift old champagne boxes in the name of love;
was calling you 'some dead woman' as if these objects you once

touched were all I claimed between us; was laughing, despite you,
with this boy you'll never meet, this boy who likes these cheeks
you handed down, who had nothing to say, he said, but held me

as if it mattered now. And I was grown up, with your face on,
heating spice after spice to smoke out the smell of books, to burn
the taste buds off this bitten tongue, avoid ever speaking of you.

The Numbers Game

Take care of the person
He/she is fragile and has a propensity to die
Look at the soft cups of their eyes, if you need any more proof

I have known a person who, in contravention of the given
      narrative, was taken down
(Reached an end point too soon)
We could not explain the circumstance which most definitely,
      factually, happened
The language showed its seams and could not help
Not at its most bald, or decorated

When a person we love is taken off it is—

1. Better and worse than we might have imagined. Better, because,
   mostly, we do not fail to go on living. Which is, after all, the
   main agenda.

      This is one kind of experience:
      You find a rope to hold
      You are on a steep incline and you drag yourself upwards
         or you hang on in stasis
      You cannot describe it except to say there is no light, your
         hands on the rope are raw and your whole body aches
      At every moment you think
      I cannot go on
      But you go on

This is one way of getting through but
As you can see   it is not very satisfactory
To pass through something is rarely unscathing
There is also getting by
Getting by is not getting through, to paraphrase a person
Who famously

2. Worse because—

3.

It might be better not to make any other suggestions.

*

I was very young when I was cracked open.

Some things you should let go of
Others you shouldn't
Views differ as to which

I kept hold of everything, just in case

*

We are trained to revere life
To look back on it at the end of a person's life and count what we have
        found of value
This is a kind of comfort
On the whole I conform to this theory
After all, what else can we do?

> *Praise be for the human spirit, and the spirits of animals,*
> *   which also soar*
> *Praise be for the gentle, brokenhearted person*

*

When the terrible thing happened someone said   Be strong
As if we might lay steel cables for bones, petrify our whole soft viscera

(The skin is a sort of protective organ and yet it is not safe from most
things, it is a jolly weak kind of coating to put on a vulnerable person.)

I repeated the phrase to someone in crisis
I do not know if they managed to achieve it

The Descent

By then the post boxes were gagged.
Fire was a controlled substance and music
was banned unilaterally. Nobody had a birthday.

I met you beneath a broken streetlamp
on Aldwych, where you once explained
Actor–Network Theory using raisins.

Fresh fruit was considered anarchic.
I've always been scared to do wrong.
We walked the wide streets through the city;

I watched your breath disperse in the frosty air
and feared I was failing at living. You led me
through an unmarked door, down stairs

that spiralled underground. The temperature rose
and the walls throbbed as we descended.
Whatever I still clung to gave way at last,

just as a floor might fall in a burning house.
Until the final step you kept your back to me.
I hardly knew you; I hardly knew myself.

Bad New Government

Love, I woke in an empty flat   to a bad new government
It was cold   the fridge was still empty   my heart, that junkie
was still chomping on the old fuel   *vroom*, I start the day like a tired
     motorcyclist   I want to go very fast and email you about the following
happy circumstances: early rosebuds, a birthday party, a new cake recipe   but
today it's hot water bottles and austerity breakfast and my toast burns in protest

     You are not here of course but you live in me like a tiny valve of a man
You light up my chambers   Later I will call to tell you about the new
     prime minister   the worrying new developments   and about how
I am writing my first political poem which is also (always) about my love for you

[57]

Acknowledgements

Thank you to the following publications or websites where some of these poems (or versions of them) previously appeared: *Ambit, Anthology for 21, Best British Poetry 2011* (Salt, 2011), *Dear World and Everyone In It* (Bloodaxe, 2012), Granta.com, Likestarlings.com, *Lung Jazz: Young British Poets for Oxfam* (Cinnamon, 2012), *Magma, Manhattan Review,* Mercyonline.co.uk, *New Statesman,* Nthposition.com, *Other Poetry, Pen Pusher, Poetry London, Poetry Review, Poetry Wales, Psycho Poetica* (Sidekick Books, 2012), *The Rialto, Rising, Smiths Knoll, Spectator, Times Literary Supplement, Stop Sharpening Your Knives 3 & 4* and *Voice Recognition: 21 Poets for the 21st Century* (Bloodaxe, 2009). A number of the poems also appeared in a pamphlet, *Stingray Fevers* (tall-lighthouse, 2008), edited by Roddy Lumsden. This collection was completed with the help of a 2008 Eric Gregory Award from the Society of Authors, and a 2010 bursary from Arts Council England, for which I am very grateful. Most of all I would like to thank: my father, family and friends; my poetry tutors; Sam Riviere, for 'austerity breakfast'; my editor, Matthew Hollis; and, particularly, Heather Phillipson and Jack Underwood.